1939　　A Time Travel's Guide: Flashback Serie

In the Embrac
A Journey Through Time

Celebrating your year
1939
A memorable year for

Content

Introduction...5

Chapter 1: The Gathering Storm: World Politics and the Outbreak of War
1.1 Poland --- Start of World War II..................................6
1.2 Leaders and Statesmen of '39....................................12
Activity: Matching the political events with their correct time..17

Chapter 2: Hollywood's Golden Year: Films and Stars
2.1 Memorable Films of 1939..18
2.2 Prestigious Film Awards..23
Activity: Movie and TV Show Trivia Quiz.............................25

Chapter 3: Sounds of Change: Music and the Pulse of 1939
3.1 Top songs of 1939..28
3.2 Renowned Musicians and Bands of '39............................32
Activity: Let's sing the song from '39..............................37

Chapter 4: Sports in 1939
Achievements and Memorable Victories in types of sport..............38
Activity: Sports Trivia - Test Your Knowledge of 1939 Sports History...43

Chapter 5: Fashion, Entertainment and Popular Leisure Activities
5.1. What the World Wore in '39....................................46
5.2 Entertainment..50
Activity: Guess fabulous '39 fashion................................64

Chapter 6: Innovations and Inventions: Technological Milestones of a Year

6.1 Technological Innovations That Shaped the Future......................65
6.2 Popular Cars Styles..69
Activity: Let's draw a picture of "car of 1939"...74

Chapter 7: The Cost of Things

The Cost of Living in 1939...76
Activity: How the life changed...80

Chapter 8: Births of 1933

Notable individuals born in 1933...82
Activity: "Profiles in Achievement: The Noteworthy
Births of 1939"...92

Special gift for readers...97
Activity answers..98

Introduction

"In the Hush of Memories: 1939's Enduring Embrace"

To all those who carry a piece of 1939 within your heart, this book is a tender tribute to the moments, the stories, and the essence that define this unforgettable year. Whether you found your first breath in its embrace, celebrated a milestone, or simply hold dear the echoes of its time, here lies a treasure trove crafted especially for you.

Within these pages, we extend an invitation to journey back to the cherished year of 1939, where history wove its intricate tales and left indelible imprints on the tapestry of time. Immersed in the gentle whispers of an era rich with significance, you'll find a collection of tales, insights, and reflections that illuminate the depth and significance of this remarkable chapter.

A careful blend of historical narratives, personal recollections, and thoughtful reflections awaits, inviting you to rediscover the joy of old memories and to bask in the poignant nostalgia that this exceptional year evokes. As you explore the depths of 1939's history and culture, may you find solace, inspiration, and a renewed connection to the vibrant threads of history that continue to enrich our lives.

With sincerity and warm regards
Edward Art Lab

Chapter 1:
World Politics and the Outbreak of War

1.1 Poland --- Start of World War II

The invasion of Poland by Nazi Germany on September 1, 1939, is widely considered the event that marked the beginning of World War II. This aggressive military action led to the subsequent involvement of various countries and the outbreak of a global conflict that would span several years and have far-reaching consequences for the world. The invasion of Poland remains a significant and tragic chapter in the history of the 20th century.

United Kingdom declaration of war on Germany

on September 3, 1939, France and the United Kingdom, along with other countries in the British Commonwealth, such as Australia, New Zealand, South Africa, and Canada, declared war on Germany in response to its invasion of Poland. This declaration of war signaled the beginning of active involvement by these nations in what would soon become known as World War II, a conflict that would eventually engulf much of the world.

Pact of Steel: Italy–Germany

The Pact of Steel, also known as the Pact of Friendship and Alliance between Germany and Italy, was a military and political alliance signed by Nazi Germany and Fascist Italy on May 22, 1939. The pact was a significant development in the lead-up to World War II and formalized the relationship between the two fascist powers.

Manhattan Project

The Manhattan Project was a research and development undertaking during World War II that produced the first nuclear weapons. It was initiated by the United States with the support of the United Kingdom and Canada. The project was a top-secret effort that led to the development of the atomic bombs that were later used in the bombings of Hiroshima and Nagasaki in Japan.

On October 11, 1939, President Franklin D. Roosevelt received a letter from physicists Albert Einstein and Leo Szilard, warning about the potential development of "extremely powerful bombs of a new type" and the necessity of conducting research into nuclear chain reactions. This letter played a significant role in the eventual start of the Manhattan Project.

Winter War

It began with a Soviet invasion of Finland on November 30, 1939. The Soviet Union sought to annex some Finnish territory, particularly in the border regions. Despite being outnumbered and outgunned, the Finns put up a determined resistance, showcasing exceptional military skill and resilience in the face of overwhelming odds. The conflict lasted for several months and concluded with the Moscow Peace Treaty in March 1940, which resulted in Finland ceding some territory to the Soviet Union.

The Winter War remains a significant event in Finnish history, demonstrating the courage and determination of the Finnish people in the face of aggression.

1.2 Leaders and Statesmen of '39

In 1939, several prominent leaders and statesmen played critical roles in shaping the course of events during a tumultuous time in world history. Some of the notable figures from that period

Franklin D. Roosevelt

Franklin D. Roosevelt was the 32nd President of the United States, serving from 1933 until his death in 1945. He is widely remembered for extend into the early years of World War II, during which he guided the nation through the challenges of the global conflict. He is often praised for his skillful diplomacy and for fostering strong international alliances, particularly with the United Kingdom and the Soviet Union, which were crucial in the eventual defeat of Nazi Germany and its allies. Roosevelt's domestic and international leadership has solidified his legacy as one of the most influential and consequential presidents in American history.

Adolf Hitler

The Chancellor of Germany and leader of the Nazi Party, whose aggressive expansionist policies and was the primary instigator of World War II.

Under Hitler's leadership, Germany invaded and occupied several countries, including Poland, France, and the Soviet Union, among others. The atrocities committed by the Nazi regime, including the Holocaust, resulted in the systematic persecution and mass murder of millions of people, making Hitler one of the most reviled figures in modern history.

Winston Churchill

In 1939, Winston Churchill remained an influential and vocal figure in British politics. He was an outspoken critic of Prime Minister Neville Chamberlain's policy of appeasement toward Nazi Germany, warning of the dangers posed by Hitler's aggressive expansionist policies. Churchill consistently advocated for a stronger and more resolute stance against the growing threat of Nazi aggression.

Furthermore, as a member of the British War Cabinet, Churchill played a key role in the strategic decisions made in the early stages of the war, providing valuable insights and guidance as the United Kingdom prepared to confront the Axis powers. His contributions in 1939 laid the groundwork for his later ascension to the position of Prime Minister, where his leadership would become synonymous with the British resistance against Nazi tyranny.

Neville Chamberlain

Neville Chamberlain served as the Prime Minister of the United Kingdom in 1939. He is best known for his policy of appeasement toward Nazi Germany, which he pursued in the years leading up to the outbreak of World War II. Chamberlain believed that by making concessions to Hitler, particularly regarding territorial expansion, he could avoid a larger conflict and maintain peace in Europe.

Benito Mussolini

Benito Mussolini, as the leader of Italy and founder of the Fascist movement, exerted significant influence on European politics during the late 1930s. Mussolini's alignment with Nazi Germany, led by Adolf Hitler, was cemented through the signing of the "Pact of Steel" in May 1939. This agreement further solidified the relationship between the two countries, creating the Axis powers' alliance, which sought to challenge the existing balance of power in Europe. Under Mussolini's leadership, Italy adopted an expansionist foreign policy, aiming to re-establish a sphere of influence in the Mediterranean and North Africa.

Activity:
Matching the political events with their correct time

Time	Event
May 22, 1939	Pact of Steel: Italy-Germany
September 3, 1939	Poland - Start of World War II
September 1, 1939	United Kingdom declaration of war on Germany
November 30, 1939 – March 13, 1940	Manhattan Project
1939–1946 (development period)	Winter War

Chapter 2: Hollywood's Golden Year: Films and Awards in 1939

2.1 Memorable Films of '39

I"Hollywood's Golden Year refers to the remarkable year of 1939 in the American film industry.

Gone with the Wind

"Gone with the Wind": Directed by Victor Fleming and based on novel of the same name Mitchell's novel, It was about the American South before and during the Civil War. The classic film "Gone With the Wind" has its debut in Atlanta, Georgia on December 15th and is often considered one of the greatest films of all time.

The Wizard of Oz

Directed by Victor Fleming, this beloved musical fantasy film, based on L. Frank Baum's novel, gained iconic status for its memorable characters, timeless songs, and innovative use of Technicolor. The film was nominated for the Academy Award for Best Picture. This colorful, creative and quotable film tops many greatest films lists and is still enjoyed by audiences today.

Mr. Smith Goes to Washington

Directed by Frank Capra, this inspiring political drama starring James Stewart explores themes of idealism, corruption, and the power of the individual in a democratic society. Its message of integrity and standing up for what is right continues to resonate with audiences.

Stagecoach

""Stagecoach," directed by John Ford, is widely regarded as one of the most influential Western films in cinematic history. Released in 1939, it marked a significant shift in the Western genre, introducing a more complex approach to character development and storytelling.

Ninotchka

"Ninotchka," directed by Ernst Lubitsch and released in 1939, is a classic romantic comedy that skillfully combines elements of romance and political satire. Starring Greta Garbo in the titular role, the film offers a humorous and nuanced exploration of the clash between Soviet Russia and the Western world during a time of political tension.

Of Mice and Men

Directed by Lewis Milestone, this film is an adaptation of John Steinbeck's 1937 novella of the same name. The story revolves around two displaced ranch workers, George and Lennie, during the Great Depression.

Wuthering Heights

Wuthering Heights is a 1939 American romantic period drama film directed by William Wyler, produced by Samuel Goldwyn, starring Merle Oberon, Laurence Olivier and David Niven, and based on the 1847 novel Wuthering Heights by Emily Brontë.

The film won the 1939 New York Film Critics Award for Best Film. It earned nominations for eight Academy Awards,[6] including for Best Picture, Best Director and Best Actor.

2.2 Prestigious Film Awards

The 12th Academy Awards, which took place in 1940, recognizing outstanding achievements in the film industry for the year 1939. Here is the breakdown of the awards:

Best Picture
"Gone with the Wind" (Producer: David O. Selznick)

Best Director: Victor Fleming for "Gone with the Wind"

Best Actor Robert Donat for "Goodbye, Mr. Chips"

Best Actress:
Vivien Leigh for "Gone with the Wind"

Best Art Direction:
Lyle R. Wheeler for "Gone with the Wind"

Best Original Story:
Lewis R. Foster for "Mr. Smith Goes to Washington"

Best Adaptation:
Sidney Howard for "Gone with the Wind"

Activity:
Movie and TV Show Trivia Quiz
How Well Do You Know '39 Entertainment?

Introduction: Let's test your knowledge of the iconic films and prestigious awards from the world of entertainment in 1939. Choose the correct answers (a, b, c, or d) for each question.

1. Which film won the Academy Award for Best Picture in 1939?

a) Gone with the Wind

b) The Wizard of Oz

c) Mr. Smith Goes to Washington

d) Wuthering Heights

2. Who won the Academy Award for Best Actor in 1939?

a) Laurence Olivier

b) Clark Gable

c) James Stewart

d) Robert Donat

3. What classic film, based on a novel by L. Frank Baum, was released in 1939, becoming one of the most beloved films in cinematic history?

a) The Wizard of Oz

b) Gone with the Wind

c) Stagecoach

d) Goodbye, Mr. Chips

4.What was the highest-grossing film of 1939?
a) Gone with the Wind
b) The Wizard of Oz
c) Stagecoach
d) Mr. Smith Goes to Washington

5.Who won the Academy Award for Best Actress in 1939?
a) Vivien Leigh
b) Bette Davis
c) Greer Garson
d) Ginger Rogers
Answer: a

6.Which acclaimed American director's film, "Stagecoach," released in 1939, is often credited with revitalizing the Western genre in Hollywood?
a) John Ford
b) Howard Hawks
c) Frank Capra
d) King Vidor

7. What American film, directed by Frank Capra, was released in 1939 and became known for its portrayal of the American political system?
a) Mr. Deeds Goes to Town
b) Meet John Doe
c) Mr. Smith Goes to Washington
d) You Can't Take It with You

8.Who won the Academy Award for Best Art Direction in 1939 for her role in the film "Gone with the Wind"?
a) Hattie McDaniel
b) Olivia de Havilland
c) Geraldine Fitzgerald
d) Lyle R. Wheeler

9.What American film, directed by John Ford, was released in 1939, telling the story of a group of stagecoach passengers traveling through dangerous Apache territory?
a) My Darling Clementine
b) She Wore a Yellow Ribbon
c) The Searchers
d) Stagecoach

10.Who received the Academy Award for Best Adaptation in 1939?
a) Sidney Howard
b) Lyle R. Wheeler
c) Herbert Stothart
d) Lewis R. Foster

Let's see how well you know the world of entertainment in 1939!

Chapter 3:
Music: Top Songs and Awards

3.1. Top songs

Here are some significant musical highlights from that year

"Over the Rainbow" - Judy Garland

This timeless classic, featured in the film "The Wizard of Oz," is one of the most beloved and recognizable songs in the history of cinema. Judy Garland's poignant rendition captured the hearts of audiences and has since become an emblem of hope and yearning.

"God Bless America" by Kate Smith

Written by Irving Berlin, "God Bless America" is a patriotic anthem that gained immense popularity during a time of political and social upheaval. Kate Smith's stirring interpretation of the song solidified its place as a symbol of American unity and pride.

"Strange Fruit" - Billie Holiday

This haunting and powerful song, originally a poem written by Abel Meeropol, highlights the horrors of racism and lynching in the American South. Billie Holiday's haunting rendition, with its stark imagery and emotional depth, made it a significant protest song of the era.

Body and Soul" - Coleman Hawkins

Regarded as a masterpiece of jazz and a landmark recording in the history of the genre, Coleman Hawkins' rendition of "Body and Soul" revolutionized the approach to the tenor saxophone in jazz music. Its emotional intensity and improvisational style have made it an enduring piece in the jazz canon.

"Deep Purple" by Larry Clinton

"Deep Purple" is a popular song that was composed by Peter DeRose, with lyrics by Mitchell Parish. Larry Clinton's version of "Deep Purple" became highly popular, featuring a smooth and romantic arrangement that resonated with audiences at the time. The song has since become a jazz standard and has been recorded by various artists in a range of musical styles.

"And the Angels Sing" by Benny Goodman

"And the Angels Sing" is a well-known song that was composed by Ziggy Elman and Johnny Mercer. The song features a lively and upbeat swing style, which was characteristic of Goodman's music. "And the Angels Sing" became one of the signature tunes for Benny Goodman and was a significant hit during the big band era. The catchy melody and memorable lyrics contributed to the song's enduring popularity, making it a staple in the repertoire of many jazz and swing bands.

3.2 Renowned Musicians and Bands of '39

In 1939, the music scene was alive with the sounds of renowned musicians and bands who made their mark on the era. Here are some of the notable figures and groups that captured the hearts of music enthusiasts in '39:

1. Benny Goodman

A celebrated jazz clarinetist and bandleader known as the "King of Swing," Goodman was a prominent figure in the swing era, and his band was one of the most popular during the late 1930s.

2. Glenn Miller

An influential trombonist, composer, and bandleader, Miller was known for his distinctive sound in both jazz and swing music. His Glenn Miller Orchestra produced several chart-topping hits in 1939.

3. Duke Ellington

A prolific composer, pianist, and bandleader, Duke Ellington was a central figure in the history of jazz. His orchestra was highly influential and produced many innovative and enduring compositions this year.

4. Artie Shaw

A renowned clarinetist, composer, and bandleader, Shaw was one of the most popular and innovative musicians of the swing era. His orchestra produced several successful recordings in 1939, contributing to his lasting impact on the genre.

5. Tommy Dorsey

A celebrated trombonist, composer, and bandleader, Tommy Dorsey led one of the most popular big bands of the era. His smooth trombone playing and the polished sound of his orchestra contributed to his widespread acclaim.

6. Billie Holiday

As a legendary jazz and blues singer, Billie Holiday's emotive voice and unique style made her one of the most influential vocalists of the era. Her song "Strange Fruit," released in 1939, remains one of her most iconic recordings. Holiday's emotive delivery and the song's powerful lyrics brought to light the horrors of racial violence and the realities of racial discrimination during that time.

7. The Andrews Sisters:

A popular vocal trio comprising sisters Patty, Maxene, and LaVerne Andrews, The Andrews Sisters were renowned for their close harmonies and successful recordings, contributing to the vibrant pop music scene of the era.

8. Jimmie Lunceford

As pioneering jazz alto saxophonist and bandleader, Jimmie Lunceford led a highly successful big band known for its polished arrangements and dynamic performances.

Activity:
Let's sing the song from '39

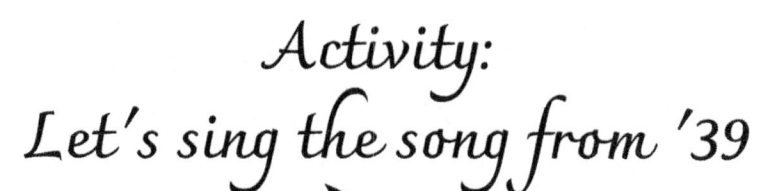

Over the Rainbow

Somewhere over the rainbow
Way up high
There's a land that I heard of
Once in a lullaby
Somewhere over the rainbow
Skies are blue
And the dreams that you dare to dream
Really do come true
Someday I'll wish upon a star
And wake up where the clouds are far behind me
Where troubles melt like lemon drops
Away above the chimney tops
That's where you'll find me
Somewhere over the rainbow
Bluebirds fly
Birds fly over the rainbow
Why then, oh, why can't I?
Somewhere over the rainbow
Bluebirds fly
Birds fly over the rainbow
Why then, oh, why can't I?
If happy little bluebirds fly
Beyond the rainbow
Why, oh why can't I?

- Judy Garland

Chapter 4: Sports in 1939:
A Journey Through the World of Athletics

4.1 Memorable Achievements and Victories

1939 was a significant year in sports, marked by several notable achievements, victories, and memorable events. From baseball to tennis, boxing to golf, cycling to football, this chapter explores the athletic feats that defined the year. the key highlights that defined the sporting landscape in 1939. Join us on a journey through a year when sports became a source of inspiration, creating legends and leaving an indelible mark on history.

Baseball

In 1939, **The New York Yankees** secured their fourth consecutive World Series championship, solidifying their place as one of the most dominant teams in baseball history. Led by their legendary player and manager, the renowned Babe Ruth, the Yankees continued to showcase exceptional skill, teamwork, and determination, captivating fans and solidifying their status as a powerhouse in the world of baseball.

Boxing Greatness

Joe Louis, also known as the "Brown Bomber," was a towering figure in the world of boxing in 1939. His exceptional skill, power, and agility in the ring set him apart as one of the most dominant and formidable heavyweight boxers of his era. During 1939, he continued to showcase his prowess and solidify his reputation as one of the greatest boxers in history.

Wimbledon Championships

The 1939 Wimbledon Championships took place in United Kingdom. Alice Marble and Bobby Riggs were awarded the Wimbledon Championships in women's and men's singles, respectively, for their outstanding performances in tennis. Their victories at the Wimbledon Championships in 1939 not only solidified their places in tennis history but also inspired future generations of tennis players, showcasing the importance of perseverance, skill, and sportsmanship in the world of professional tennis.

US Golf Open

Byron Nelson, a legendary figure in the world of golf, indeed made a significant impact in 1939 with his exceptional performances, securing victories at the United States Open Golf Championship. Nelson's remarkable achievements cemented his reputation as one of the most skilled and accomplished golfers of his time, leaving an indelible mark on the sport.

Masters Tournament

Ralph Guldahl achieved considerable success, including winning the Masters Tournament, which was then known as the Augusta National Invitational, in both 1939 and 1940.

Guldahl's victories at the Masters Tournament were indicative of his exceptional skill, precision, and strategic play on the golf course. Ralph Guldahl was indeed a prominent figure in the world of golf during the 1930s.

British Open

Richard Burton is mainly remembered for winning The Open Championship (British Open) in July 1939, when it was played on the Old Course at St Andrews in Scotland

Ice Hockey World Championships

The 1939 Ice Hockey World Championships were held between February 3 and February 12, 1939, in Switzerland with Canada win.

Activity: Sports Trivia

Test Your Knowledge of 1933 Sports History

Let's choose right answer for the memorable sports events and champions from this era.

1. Who was the winner of the 1939 Wimbledon Championships men's singles title?

a) Fred Perry

b) John Bromwich

c) Don Budge

d) Bunny Austin

2. Which boxer held the world heavyweight boxing title for the majority of the 1930s, including 1939?

a) Rocky Marciano

b) Joe Louis

c) Max Baer

d) Jack Dempsey

3. In which sport did Byron Nelson excel, winning major championships in 1939?

a) Golf

b) Tennis

c) Baseball

d) Basketball

4.Who won the MLB World Series in 1939?
a) New York Yankees
b) St. Louis Cardinals
c) Cincinnati Reds
d) Chicago Cubs

5.In 1939, which city hosted the World Heavyweight Boxing Championship fight between Joe Louis and Tony Galento?
a) New York City
b) Chicago
c) Washington, D.C.
d) Jersey City

6.In 1939, which athlete set a world record in the men's 800 meters that remained unbroken for more than eight years?
a) John Woodruff
b) Ralph Metcalfe
c) Glenn Cunningham
d) Bill Bonthron

7. Which team won the 1939 Stanley Cup, the championship trophy of the National Hockey League (NHL)?
a) Boston Bruins
b) Toronto Maple Leafs
c) Detroit Red Wings
d) New York Rangers

8.In 1939, which country hosted the Men's Ice Hockey World Championships?

a) Switzerland

b) Sweden

c) Czechoslovakia

d) Canada

Enjoy the multiple-choice quiz and see how well you remember the exciting sports history of 1939!

Chapter 5: Pop Culture, Fashion, and Popular Leisure Activities

5.1 Rewind Fashion: What the World Wore in '39

In 1939, fashion around the world was influenced by a combination of the economic hardships of the Great Depression and the approach of World War II. Here is a glimpse of what the world wore in '39

Women's fashion:

1. Soft and feminine looks

Women's fashion was characterized by elegant, flowing silhouettes, with bias-cut gowns and tailored suits becoming fashionable choices.

2. Flowing dresses

Dresses were typically long, flowing, and elegant, often made of satin, velvet, or silk. The popular styles included bias-cut gowns and dresses with intricate draping. Darker hues such as deep blues, purples, and greens were commonly worn, reflecting the sobering mood of the time.

3. Hairstyles

Soft waves, curls, and updos were popular hairstyles during this year. Women often styled their hair to create the appearance of volume, with some opting for short bobs or pin curls. Headscarves and decorative hair accessories were also commonly worn.

4. Pump - Peep toe shoes

Women's shoes featured classic pumps and peep-toe styles. These elegant and often heeled shoes completed the sophisticated appearance.

5. Accessories

Women often accessorized with gloves, pearls, and costume jewelry. Hats were an essential part of women's fashion, ranging from small berets to large-brimmed hats adorned with feathers, ribbons, or artificial flowers. Handbags were typically small and structured, matching the overall style of the outfit.

Men

1. Oversized suit

Men's fashion saw the rise of the zoot suit, characterized by its oversized, broad-shouldered design.

2. Oxfords - Wingtip shoes

Oxfords: Oxfords were one of the most popular shoe styles for men in 1939. They were characterized by their closed lacing system, low heels, and a sleek, formal appearance. Oxfords were often made from leather and came in various shades of brown and black.

3. Accessories

Headwear was essential in 1933, with men often seen wearing fedora hats for a formal look or newsboy caps for a more relaxed style.

Briefcases:
Leather briefcases were a common accessory for businessmen and professionals, providing a stylish and practical way to carry documents and other essentials.

5.2. Entertainment

In 1939, entertainment was characterized by a mix of various forms of media and cultural events that reflected the social and political landscape of the time. Some of the notable entertainment characteristics of 1939 include:

Cinema:

The year 1939 is widely regarded as one of the most significant in the history of Hollywood cinema, often referred to as the "Golden Year of Hollywood." During this time, the film industry produced several iconic and timeless movies that continue to captivate audiences with their cinematic magic.

Music:

Music in 1939 was characterized by a rich variety of genres and styles, ranging from jazz and swing to classical and folk music.

Golden Age of Radio

In 1939, radio shows were a primary source of entertainment for many households. Popular shows like "The Shadow," "The Lone Ranger," and "The Jack Benny Program" captivated audiences with their thrilling storylines and engaging performances.

The Adventures of Ellery Queen

The Adventures of Ellery Queen was a radio detective program in the United States with the first one broadcast on CBS on June 18, 1939. "The Adventures of Ellery Queen" was one of the early successful detective programs in the history of radio broadcasting and contributed to the rise of detective and mystery genres in both radio and later television programming.

Golden Age of Radio
The Lone Ranger

"The Lone Ranger," based on the character created by Fran Striker, centered on the adventures of a masked Texas Ranger who fought injustice in the American Old West. It became one of the most enduring and iconic radio shows of the time, later transitioning to other forms of media, including television and film.

Dance

In the world of dance in 1939, influential figures such as Martha Graham, Doris Humphrey, and Charles Weidman were making strides in modern dance, contributing to the development of innovative choreography and movement techniques.

Launch of Batman

The superhero character Batman made his debut in Detective Comics on 27th in May 1939, marking the beginning of a cultural phenomenon that would evolve into one of the most popular and enduring comic book franchises in history.

Books published in 1939

One significant book that was published in 1939 is "**The Grapes of Wrath**" by John Steinbeck. The book won the National Book Award and Pulitzer Prize for fiction. It played a significant role in his eventual Nobel Prize in Literature in 1962. This book remains a staple of American literature and is widely studied in schools and universities around the world.

Books published in 1939

And Then There Were None

"And Then There Were None" is a mystery novel by Agatha Christie, first published in 1939 under the title "Ten Little Niggers" in the United Kingdom. The book is considered one of Christie's masterpieces and is renowned for its intricate plot, psychological tension, and unpredictable twists, which have captivated readers for generations. It is one of the best-selling mystery books of all time and has been adapted into various films, television shows, and stage productions.

Books published in 1939

Madeline

"Madeline," the classic children's book written and illustrated by Ludwig Bemelmans, has had a profound influence on children's literature and popular culture since its publication in 1939.

The Big Sleep

"The Big Sleep" is a classic hardboiled crime novel written by Raymond Chandler. It was first published in 1939 and is the first novel to feature the famous private detective Philip Marlowe. It has not only inspired numerous adaptations in film, television, and radio but has also had a lasting influence on the crime fiction genre, shaping the development of noir literature and contributing to the rise of the tough, disillusioned detective archetype in popular culture.

Books published in 1939

The Day of the Locust

"The Day of the Locust" by Nathanael West: A novel set in Hollywood during the Great Depression, it explores the dark side of the American Dream and the entertainment industry. It is known for its vivid portrayal of the desperation and disillusionment of the characters. The novel's sharp critique of the American society and its examination of the human psyche in the face of desperation have cemented its place as a notable work in American literature.

Painting Art

The Two Fridas (Las dos Fridas)
by DR. DORIS MARIA-REINA BRAVO "
The Two Fridas" has become an iconic symbol of Kahlo's introspective and deeply personal artistic expression.

Photography

During 1939, photography continued to play a crucial role in documenting significant historical events and everyday life. Photojournalism, in particular, gained prominence as photographers captured compelling and impactful images, contributing to the spread of visual storytelling and the documentation of crucial moments in history

USA Photographs 1939

Board Games and Card Games

Playing board games and card games at home was a popular form of entertainment and socializing. Games such as Monopoly, Scrabble, and various card games provided a way for families and friends to bond and enjoy leisure time together.

Share your 1939 photos,
Don't forget to show off your fabulous '39 fashion

Activity:
Guess fabulous '39 fashion

Activity:
Guess fabulous '39 fashion

Find image representing the fashion of 1939

A

B

C

Chapter 6:
Technological Advancements and Popular Cars

6.1 Innovations That Shaped the Future

The year 1939 was marked by several groundbreaking technological advancements that laid the foundation for future developments. These innovations not only contributed to scientific progress but also shaped the way people lived and enjoyed their leisure time.

Electron Microscope - Germany by Ernst Ruska:

In 1933, German scientist Ernst Ruska made significant strides in electron microscopy. The electron microscope was a revolutionary invention that allowed researchers to examine objects at an unprecedented level of detail. By using a beam of electrons to illuminate the object, the electron microscope surpassed the limitations of traditional light microscopes, enabling scientists to view structures at the nanoscale. This innovation had a profound impact on various scientific fields, including biology, materials science, and nanotechnology.

Hewlett-Packard Company Created

Hewlett-Packard (HP) is a well-known American multinational information technology company that was indeed founded in January of 1939. They created the company with just $538.00 while working together part-time in a rented garage in Palo Alto, California. The first product they created was a device called resistance-capacitance audio oscillators and were used to test sound equipment.

Frequency Modulation USA by Edwin H Armstrong

In 1939, Edwin H. Armstrong, an American electrical engineer and inventor, is credited with the invention of frequency modulation. FM was a significant improvement over amplitude modulation (AM) in terms of its resistance to static and interference, as well as its ability to deliver clearer sound quality over longer distances. Armstrong's work in radio communication and his development of FM played a crucial role in the advancement of radio technology.

The world's first helicopter by Igor Sikorsky

September 14, 1939, marked a significant milestone in the history of aviation when Igor Sikorsky's VS-300 helicopter took its first flight in Stratford, Connecticut. The VS-300 was the world's first practical helicopter, incorporating a single main rotor and tail rotor design, which has become the standard configuration for modern helicopters.

6.2 The Automobiles of '39

The automotive industry saw continued progress in 1939 with the introduction of improved designs and features in various vehicle models. Innovations in automotive engineering and manufacturing techniques paved the way for the development of more efficient and reliable cars, setting the stage for the modern automobile industry.

Austin 8

The Austin 8 was indeed a small car produced by the British manufacturer Austin Motor Company. It Launched on 24 February 1939 and known for its simple design and practicality, making it a popular choice for many families during its production period

Austin 12

The Austin 12 was indeed a large four-door family saloon produced by Austin Motor Company. Launched in August 1939, the Austin 12 was designed to cater to the needs of larger families and those seeking a more spacious and comfortable vehicle. Its launch occurred just before the outbreak of World War II, which significantly impacted the production and availability of civilian automobiles during the war years.

The Ford Model 91

The Ford Model 91 was indeed a car produced by Ford UK in 1939. It was a popular car known for its durability, reliability, and practicality, particularly during the challenging years of World War II. The Ford Model 91 and its variants played a significant role in providing transportation for families and individuals during a period of economic and social change

DKW F8

The DKW F8 was a small car produced by the German manufacturer DKW (Auto Union) was introduced in 1939. The DKW F8 was known for its compact size and economical design, making it a popular choice among consumers looking for an affordable and practical vehicle during the pre-war and wartime period. The DKW F8 offered an efficient and reliable mode of transportation for many individuals and families.

1939 BMW 335

The BMW 335 is an automobile that was produced by the German automaker BMW in 1939. It was part of the BMW 3 Series and was a successor to the BMW 326. The BMW 335 was a luxury car known for its advanced engineering and high-performance capabilities during its time.

Activity:
Let's draw a picture of "car of 1939"

Let's coloring a picture of "car of 1939"

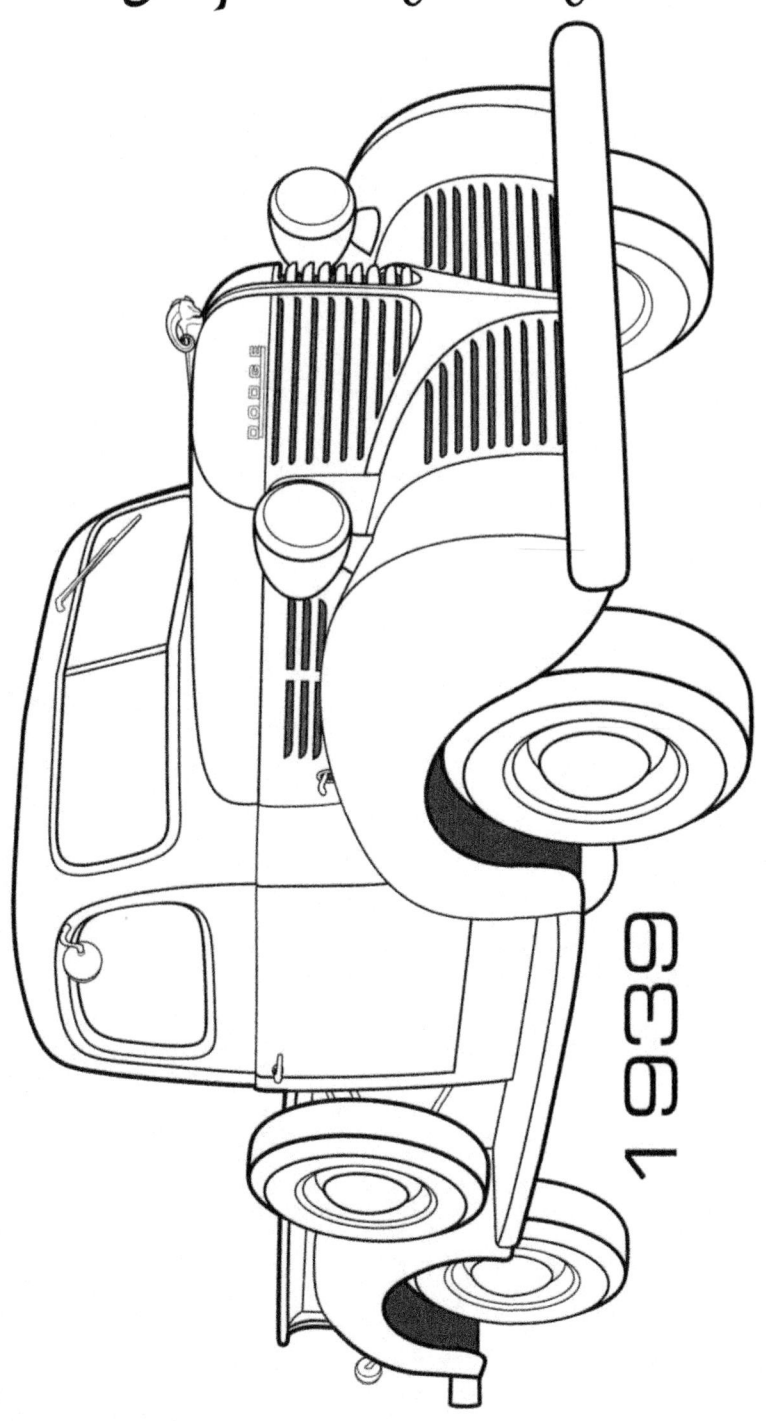

Chapter 7: The Cost of Things

HOW MUCH YOU SPEND IN 1939

Cost of Living in 1939

The year 1939 was a significant year in history, being the onset of World War II, which greatly impacted the global economy. Here are some key aspects related to the cost of living during this period:

- Average Cost of new house $3,800.00
- Average wages per year $1,730.00
- Average Monthly Rent $28.00 per month

Cost of Living in 1939

- Cost of a gallon of Gas 10 cents

- Average Price for new car $700.0

Cost of Living in 1939
Food

- A LB of Hamburger Meat 14 cents

A loaf of Bread 8 cents

Toaster $16.00

Activity:
How the life changed

Write your cost of living at the present

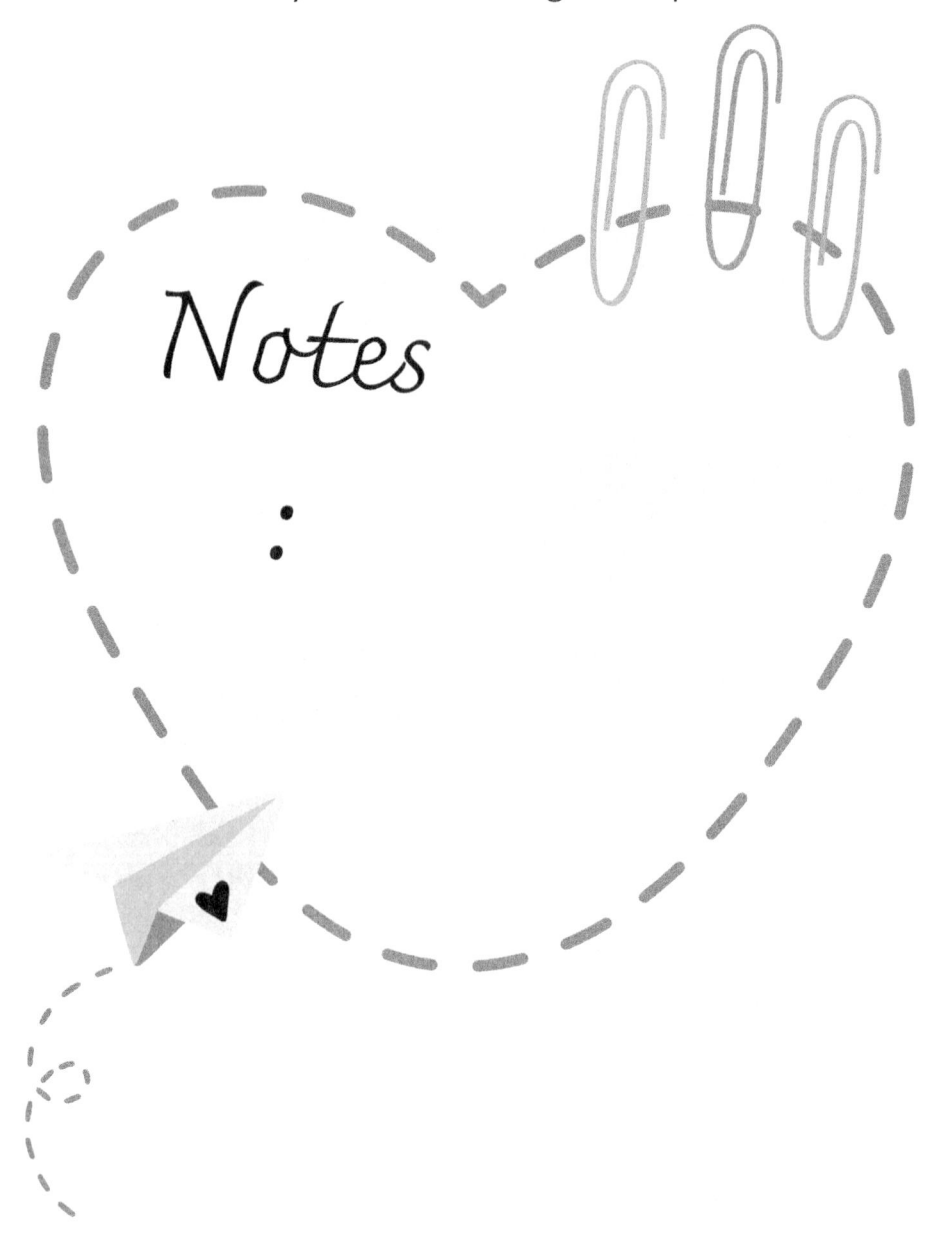

Notes

Comparing prices from 1939 with the cost of similar items in the present day. Reflect on the changes in consumer behavior

Chapter 8: Births in 1939

To the esteemed individuals born in the year 1939, their talents and contributions have left an indelible mark on the world. Their creativity, dedication, and perseverance have enriched the lives of many and inspired countless others. Several notable individuals were born in 1939. Here are some of them:

1. Francis Ford Coppola

Francis Ford Coppola, born on April 7, 1939, in Detroit, Michigan, is one of the most celebrated American film directors, producers, and screenwriters. He is widely recognized for his masterful work on "The Godfather" trilogy, which is considered one of the greatest achievements in the history of cinema. He was a central figure in the New Hollywood filmmaking movement of the 1960s and 1970s. Throughout his career, Coppola has been the recipient of multiple prestigious awards, including several Academy Awards and Golden Globe Awards, in recognition of his influential contributions to the art of filmmaking. He is considered one of the most significant and visionary filmmakers in the history of cinema.

2. Ian McKellen

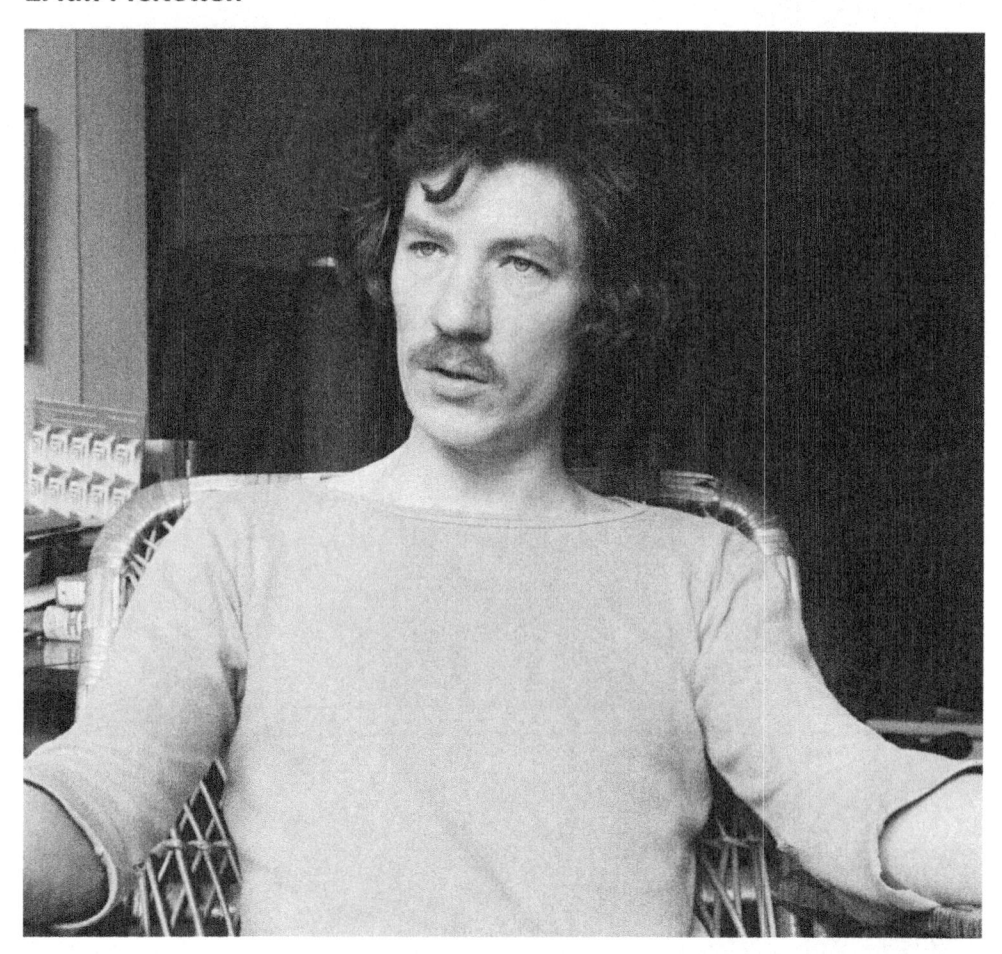

Ian McKellen, born on May 25, 1939, in England, is a highly respected British actor renowned for his versatile and powerful performances on both stage and screen. He has made significant contributions to the world of film, television, and theater throughout his illustrious career. McKellen is widely recognized for his portrayal of Gandalf in Peter Jackson's "The Lord of the Rings" film trilogy (2001-2003), based on J.R.R. Tolkien's epic fantasy novels. He is regarded as a British cultural icon and was knighted by Queen Elizabeth II in 1991. His compelling portrayal of the wise and enigmatic wizard solidified his status as a beloved figure in contemporary pop culture.

3. Marvin Gaye

Marvin Gaye, born on April 2, 1939, in Washington, D.C., was a legendary American singer, songwriter, and record producer who made significant contributions to the genres of soul, R&B, and Motown music. He is widely regarded as one of the most influential and talented musicians in the history of popular music.

4. Clive James

Clive James, born on October 7, 1939, in Kogarah, New South Wales, Australia, was a prolific and versatile figure known for his work as an author, critic, broadcaster, poet, translator, and memoirist. He gained widespread recognition for his contributions to literature and the arts, as well as his engaging and insightful commentary on various cultural and social topics.

Having moved to the United Kingdom in 1962, Clive James became a prominent figure in the British literary and media scene. He was well-known for his literary criticism and cultural commentary, often showcasing his wit and humor in his writings and broadcasts. His work encompassed various genres

5. John Cleese

John Cleese, born on October 27, 1939, in Weston-super-Mare, Somerset, England, is an esteemed English actor, comedian, and writer. He is best known for his influential contributions to the groundbreaking comedy group Monty Python and for his iconic portrayal of Basil Fawlty in the television series "Fawlty Towers."His contributions to the world of comedy have left an indelible mark on popular culture, and his wit and humor continue to resonate with audiences worldwide.

6. Tina Turner

Tina Turner, whose real name is Anna Mae Bullock, was born on November 26, 1939, in Nutbush, Tennessee, United States. She is an iconic American-born Swiss singer, songwriter, and actress, known for her powerful voice, dynamic stage presence, and career that has spanned several decades. Throughout her career, Tina Turner has received numerous awards and accolades, including multiple Grammy Awards, and has sold over 100 million records worldwide, making her one of the best-selling music artists of all time. Her electrifying stage performances and her ability to infuse soul, rock, and pop music have cemented her legacy as one of the most influential and revered figures in the history of popular music

7. James Fox

James Fox, born on May 19, 1939, in London, England, is a distinguished English actor with a career spanning several decades. He has established himself as a versatile performer, known for his compelling portrayals in film, television, and theater.His enduring presence in the entertainment industry has made him a highly respected figure in British and international cinema.

8. Paul Hogan

Paul Hogan, born on October 8, 1939, in Lightning Ridge, New South Wales, Australia, is a renowned Australian actor, comedian, and television presenter. He gained international fame for his portrayal of the character Mick "Crocodile" Dundee in the "Crocodile" Dundee film series. Hogan's contributions to the entertainment industry have solidified his status as a beloved and iconic figure, both in Australia and internationally. His portrayal of the charming and adventurous Crocodile Dundee character remains one of the most memorable and enduring in the history of Australian cinema.

9. Ayatollah Ali Khamenei

Ayatollah Ali Khamenei, born on July 17, 1939, in Mashhad, Iran, is a prominent Iranian political and religious figure. He has served as the Supreme Leader of Iran since 1989, following the death of the Islamic Republic's founder, Ayatollah Ruhollah Khomeini. As the Supreme Leader, Ayatollah Khamenei holds the highest ranking political and religious authority in the country. He is considered the ultimate decision-maker on matters of state, including domestic and foreign policy, national security, and overall governance. His leadership has significantly shaped Iran's political landscape and its relations with other countries.

10. Michael Moorcock

Michael Moorcock, born on December 18, 1939, in London, England, is a highly acclaimed and influential British writer and musician. He is best known for his prolific contributions to the science fiction and fantasy genres, having produced a vast and diverse body of work that has had a significant impact on the literary world. Moorcock received various prestigious awards, including the World Fantasy Award, the Bram Stoker Award, and the British Fantasy Award, among others, in recognition of his significant contributions to the science fiction and fantasy genres. His works have inspired generations of readers and writers, solidifying his status as one of the most influential and revered figures in the realm of speculative fiction.

Activity:
"Profiles in Achievement: The Noteworthy Births of 1939"

1. What is Tina Turner's birthdate?
a) November 26th
b) September 5th
c) April 23rd
d) July 17th

2. Marvin Gaye is renowned for his contributions to which music genres?
a) Country and folk
b) Jazz and blues
c) Soul and R&B
d) Rock and metal

3. When was Marvin Gaye born?
a) April 7th
b) April 2nd
c) October 8th
d) May 31st

4. Ginger Baker, known for his innovative drumming style, was a member of which influential rock band?
a) Led Zeppelin
b) The Beatles
c) *Cream*
d) The Rolling Stones

5. In which genre has Ian McKellen made significant contributions?
a) Horror
b) Romance
c) Science Fiction
d) Fantasy

6. Which city was James Fox born in?
a) London, England
b) Paris, France
c) Rome, Italy
d) Madrid, Spain

7. What is the birthdate of Francis Ford Coppola?
a) April 7th
b) August 12th
c) October 18th
d) July 15th

8. Which iconic film series is Francis Ford Coppola best known for directing?
a) Star Wars
b) The Godfather
c) Harry Potter
d) Jurassic Park

9. Tina Turner is known for her powerful voice in which music genre?
a) Country
b) Rock
c) Pop
d) R&B

10. Paul Hogan gained international fame for his portrayal of which iconic Australian character?
a) Crocodile Dundee
b) Mad Max
c) Ned Kelly
d) The Man from Snowy River

Do you know Celebrities Born in 1939?

We have heartfelt thank-you gifts for you

As a token of our appreciation for joining us on this historical journey through 1939, we've included a set of cards and stamps inspired by the year of 1939. These cards are your canvas to capture the essence of the past. We encourage you to use them as inspiration for creating your own unique cards, sharing your perspective on the historical moments we've explored in this book. Whether it's a holiday greeting or a simple hello to a loved one, these cards are your way to connect with the history we've uncovered together.

Happy creating!

Activity Answers

Chapter 1

Time	Event
May 22, 1939	Pact of Steel: Italy-Germany
September 3, 1939	United Kingdom declaration of war on Germany
September 1, 1939	Poland - Start of World War II
1939–1946 (development period)	Manhattan Project
November 30, 1939 – March 13, 1940	Winter War

Chapter 2:
1. a) Gone with the Wind
2. d) Robert Donat
3. a) The Wizard of Oz
4. a) Gone with the Wind
5. a) Vivien Leigh
6. a) John Ford
7. c) Mr. Smith Goes to Washington
8. d) Lyle R. Wheeler
9. d) Stagecoach
10. a) Sidney Howard

Chapter 4:
1. c) Don Budge
2. b) Joe Louis
3. a) Golf
4. a) New York Yankees
5. d) Jersey City
6. a) John Woodruff
7. c) Detroit Red Wings
8. b) Sweden

Chapter 5:
B

Chapter 8:
1. b) November 26th
2. c) Soul and R&B
3. d) April 2nd
4. c) Cream
5. d) Fantasy
6. a) London, England
7. c) April 7th
8. b) The Godfather
9. b) Rock
10. a) Crocodile Dundee

Embracing 1939: A Grateful Farewell

Honoring 1939: An Appreciative Reflection

We extend our heartfelt gratitude to you for being part of this exploration into the significant events of 1939. Whether you directly experienced the year or immersed yourself through the narrative of this book, we trust it has evoked cherished moments, nostalgia, and a deeper connection to a time that remains etched in our collective memories.

Share Your Thoughts and Help Us Preserve History

Your engagement and support have been invaluable throughout this journey. We invite you to share your insights, leave a review, and contribute to the preservation of the rich history encapsulated in the essence of '39. As we bring this journey to a close, we eagerly anticipate more expeditions through the tapestries of history together. Until then, thank you for being part of our cherished journey.

Copyright © Edward Art Lab

All rights reserved. No part of this publication may be reproduced, distributed, or transmitted in any form or by any means, including photocopying, recording, or other electronic or mechanical methods, without the prior written permission of the publisher, except in the case of brief quotations embodied in critical reviews and certain other noncommercial uses permitted by copyright law.

Happy Birthday
note

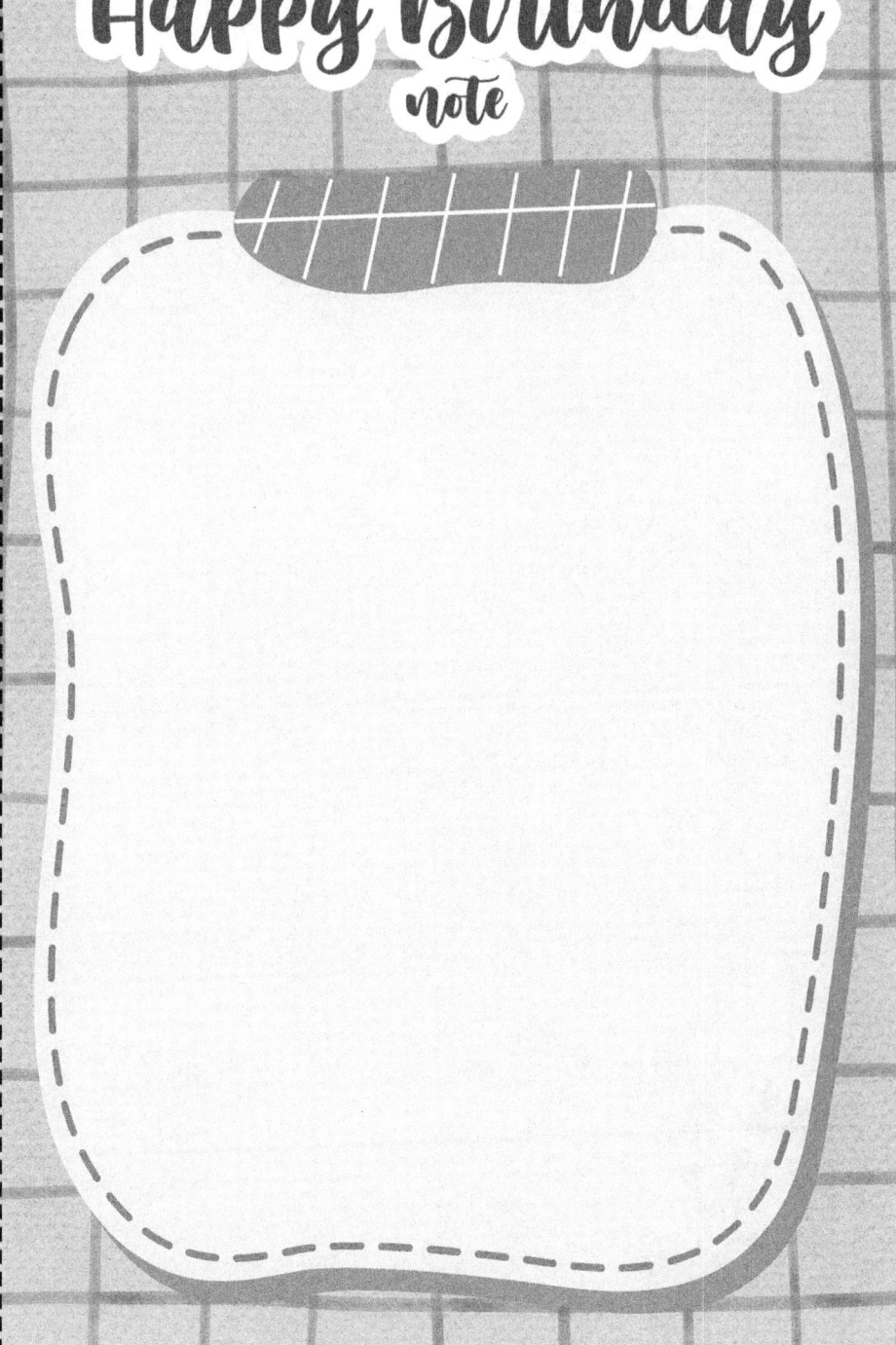

Happy Birthday
note

Happy Birthday
note

Happy Birthday
note

TO DO LIST

○ ----
○ ----
○ ----
○ ----
○ ----
○ ----
○ ----
○ ----
○ ----
○ ----
○ ----
○ ----
○ ----
○ ----

well done!

To Do List

TO DO LIST

Name: _____   Day: _____   Month: _____

No	To Do List	Yes	No

TO DO LIST

Name: _____ Day: _____ Month: _____

No	To Do List	Yes	No

TO DO LIST

Name: _____ Day: _____ Month: _____

No	To Do List	Yes	No

NOTE

NOTE

NOTE

N
W
E
S
Greetings!
TIME TO
TRAVEL
2
PACIFIC OCEAN
MAP OF
THE WORLD

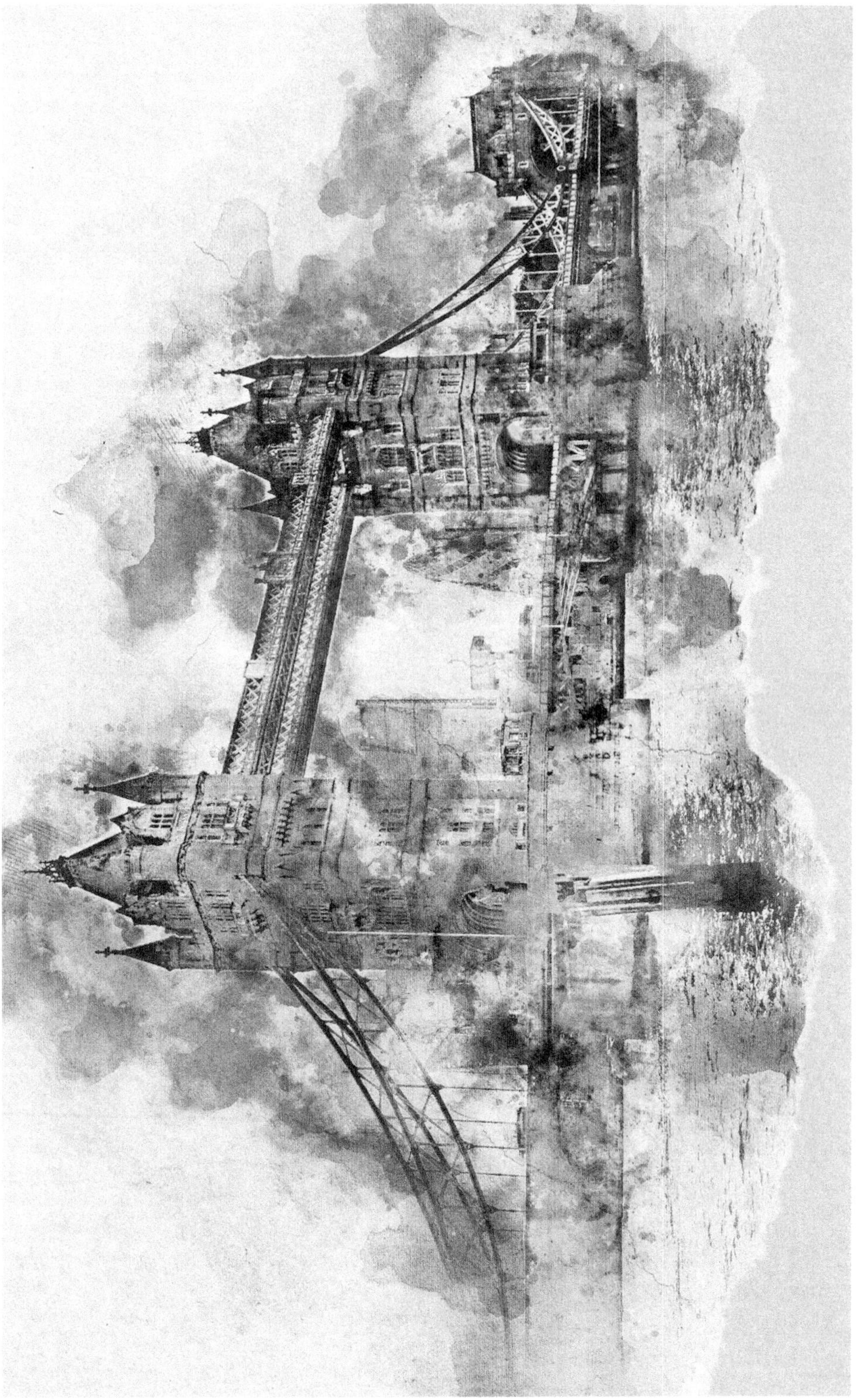

To

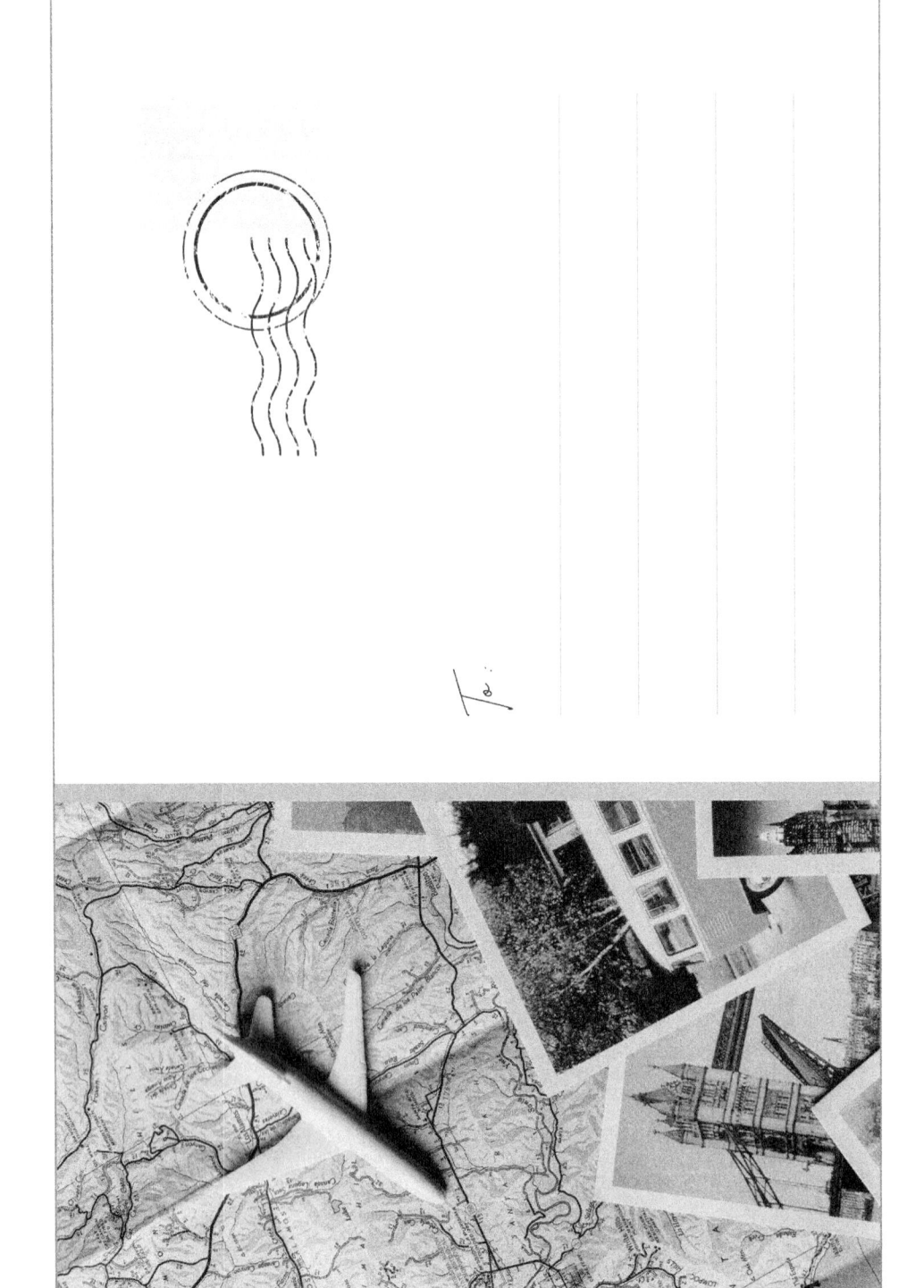

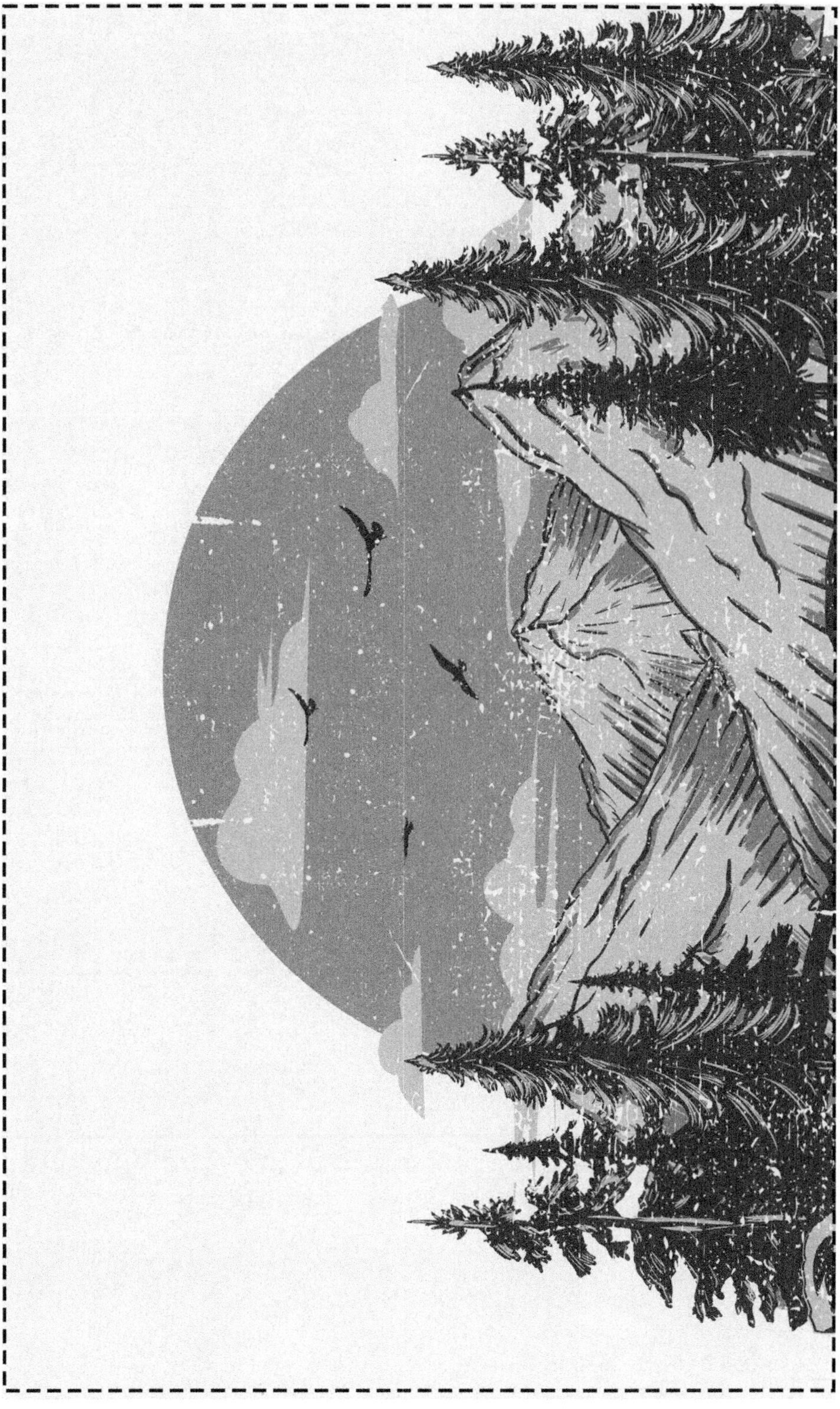

POSTCARD

To:

From:

Remember This!

WISH YOU WERE HERE,
123 ANYWHERE ST., ANY CITY

HAPPY BIRTHDAY NOTE

To Do List

- [ ] _____
- [ ] _____
- [ ] _____
- [ ] _____
- [ ] _____
- [ ] _____
- [ ] _____
- [ ] _____
- [ ] _____
- [ ] _____
- [ ] _____
- [ ] _____
- [ ] _____
- [ ] _____